Matt Fielder is a prolific writer who has previously had work published as a food critic, columnist and journalist for *The Richmond and Twickenham Times*, as well as just about every other local newspaper and magazine in Surrey. He is also a renowned compère and MC of many events both large and small up and down the country, as well as an accomplished kids and adult party DJ. He is, however, perhaps best known locally for being a rock singer and fronting many bands over the years. He currently has an album out *21-Gun Salute* by the United Kingdom of Rock, showcasing his work and gigs regularly on the pub circuit with classic rock cover band *Ransom*. He has been married for 30 years to his wife, Alicia, and they have two children – Ryan (16) and Zosia (11) – and they live in Fetcham, Surrey. Although a contributor to many publications over the years, this is in fact his first officially published book of any description.

To Sarah,
thank you
for your patience
in waiting for fella!
lots of love

To my beautiful, long-suffering wife, Alicia, of nearly 30 amazing years who still rocks my world. My two incredibly talented, independent and constantly inspirational children, Ryan and Zosia. To my band, *Ransom*, and all my Rock 'n' Roll family throughout the years. To my ever-increasing and sadly (in some places) diminishing pool of family and friends everywhere, you all know who you are and what you did and I am now and forevermore eternally grateful to you. To Howard Smith at No Sloppy Copy for being a such good friend and running his trained eyes and grammatical ruler over my work and making the necessary suggestions and alterations where applicable. i.e. 'sticking in all the commas and shit'. To all the brave NHS and key workers who are currently helping keep us all alive right now and to everyone who has ever believed in me. Finally, a big shout out goes to anyone who may be reading this and thinking I may have forgotten them, I haven't…and thank you.

Matt Fielder

A Life in a Calendar Year

Austin Macauley Publishers™

LONDON • CAMBRIDGE • NEW YORK • SHARJAH

A CIP catalogue record for this title is available from the British Library.

ISBN 9781528998260 (Paperback)
ISBN 9781528998277 (ePub e-book)

www.austinmacauley.com

First Published (2020)
Austin Macauley Publishers Ltd
25 Canada Square
Canary Wharf
London
E14 5LQ

Thanks to Kay and everyone at Austin Macauley Publishers, the late, great Hugh McIlvanney for the inspiration and laying down the gauntlet, "Matthew, there are people who say and people who do." To my best mate of forty-odd years (his son) Conn, to Tom D for always saying, "Get your work published." And finally, to Alicia…I fed my soul baby and just look what happened!

January

So New Year's now upon us
For some, a fresh, new start
To wipe away the memories
That are tearing them apart

For all those resolutions
Here comes a brand-new me
So many empty promises
Made by my Christmas tree

A fit and healthy lifestyle
Beginning from day one
A dry and smoke-free January
A workout, swim or run

Give up on social media
And see who really cares
(But sneak a peek occasionally
Keep tabs on likes and shares)

Holding out till February
To show you give a damn
For once the frost has settled
The toys 'll be in their pram

For some it lasts much longer
So determined to succeed
Reaping whirlwinds of prosperity
As resentment will recede

For the only real lesson
That we ever truly learn
Is that time's the only healer
Not the calories we burn.

Written on 1 January 2018 in the Moravian mountains in the Czech Republic and dedicated to all those New-Year, New-Me folk.

February

Is there a vision, is there a call?
Is there a light that defines us all?
Have we a purpose or is it just fate?
Is it all pre-determined – how long we must wait

For some kind of signal to show us the way
To lead us from darkness, keep demons at bay?
There must be a reason why we're all here
A road to redemption that makes it all clear

All the fussing and fighting, divisions of hate
That argue the path to their heaven's gate
The Garden of Eden, some divine, holy right
The fruit of temptation that leads us to bite
But all of these preaching and all of the prayers

Stretch the fabric of truth until it just tears
So what do we teach, these kids of today
What guidance do we have so they're not led astray?

There isn't an app that connects them to God
No cast to download to their mini iPod
Instead it is nature, the birds and the trees
The wind and the rain and the colour of leaves

It's what I show mine whenever I can
For I truly believe there's a much-wider plan
Life will continue long after we're gone
And our shadows will fade once our sun has shone

On this February day, there's a cold, winter chill
As reality bites like the bitterest pill
So let's just leave something to show we were here
Then off to the pub for some coke, crisps and beer!

Written outside the Stephan Langton Inn, Abinger, near Dorking, Surrey, having just returned from Safari in the Kruger National Park, South Africa. There was grief at work, Money was tight and it was February, 'the Tuesday of the calendar months', and my thoughts were with everyone pondering the meaning of life.

March

No one compares to all that you are
The things that you do, both near and afar
You're the rock on which this home is built
The gift from above that bears no guilt

Always striving to do what is best
As you wash and clean and feather our nest
You ask for nothing but the respect that is due
But we are the ones who haven't a clue

How to pay back the debt that we owe
The depth of our love we can never show
Flowers, chocolates and cards are all fine
Jewellery, perfumes or bottles of wine

For you are our mother who stands out alone
And we thank you forever for all you have shown
We know we're not worthy but on this special day
We *will* try to do whatever you say

The Mad March Hare's tea party's begun
Through looking-glass eyes we commence all the fun
Daffodils are picked and cards are displayed
Now Lord help you with the breakfast they've made!

Written on Mother's Day in March 2018 as the kids 'prepared' breakfast for their mum. This is an archive picture but is sums up the mayhem and chaos of that morning – and of many others previously!

April

So I'm riding the waves of being just me
Surfing the tides that set my spirit free
Rocking, laughing, living the dream
Yet never forgetting I'm part of a team

Loyalty, trust, happiness and hope
Dealing with more than many could cope
Making the effort where others won't go
Believing in things they can never know

Trying to stay true to all that I am
Fire of the dragon, horn of the ram
Mars is my ruler, diamond my stone
Rock my religion from core to the bone

Big Celtic heart with full English blood
I am the bull that's been put out to stud
So love me, leave me, do as you must
But I am the metal that will never rust

And I'll keep on coming till I am no more
Beating the count from the canvas floor
Dismiss me at peril, cos I won't go away
I'll still be smiling come my judgement day

It ain't about money, position or wealth
The cards I'm dealt or the state of my health
For I know the score, the meaning of life
My kids, my friends, my band and my wife

The showers of April give way to the sun
I'm in the zone, my time has begun
Being at one with nature and all
I know who I am and I've answered my call!

Written for my birthday in April, this is the rattling, sabre cry of someone not ready to be put out to pasture just yet. My mood was reflective as I sat cooking sausages on an open fire somewhere in Norway.

May

Never post your opinion until you've thought it through
Or prepare for the backlash that surely will ensue
Don't let total strangers ever give it to you straight
Cos we're all keyboard warriors when rising to the bait

Never brag about your team, no matter what the score
Cos it'll come back to haunt you, win, lose or draw
Avoid washing laundry in view of public glare
You never know who is watching at what it is you share

Try not to get offended with everything you see
Just learn to live and let live, as what will be, will be
Forget the cryptic comments of the attention-seeking kind
When you're angry, hurt and upset or in a bad state of mind

'That's it, I'm done, you asked for this and now
you're gonna pay!'
'Inbox me babes, I'm here for you, what's the gossip of the
day?'
Everyone's fighting battles no one else understands
Scrambling to meet their deadlines through time's shifting
sands

No one has the patience to listen anymore
To find out what's really going on outside of their front door
Jumping to conclusions, as ignorance is bliss
Can you really do the telling if you didn't see the kiss?

Politics and religion are like red rags to a bull
For the baying crowds, thirst for blood won't stop until it's
full
So never play the victim or exaggerate the crime
As one side of the story won't wash out all the grime

The truth will out soon enough, just like the midday sun
So take it all in context as just a bit of fun
Cos May Day's here and I can feel that spring is in the air
Deliberate, ignore the hate and pretend that you don't care.

*It was May and the sun was shining gloriously. Yet all I
could see on Facebook were people fighting with each
other. #toomuchhate. Then I came across this photo of my*

son gazing out over the Grand Canyon. It made me realise how little impact, in the grand scheme of things, people's petty squabbles on social media really have on the world.

June

We take our choices, we make our beds
We follow the nonsense in our heads
Crossing wires and forming mesh
Give in to desires of the flesh

Breaking hearts and stealing souls
Building fences without the poles
No ground is truer than that where we stand
But still we preach what we don't understand

Opinions differ on every street
Suspicions rise on all we meet
Conspiracists rage and scream at you
That what you believe just cannot be true

Distorting 'facts' to back up their claim
They belittle their targets and then take aim
They're trying to convince both you and me
Whilst scoring points off some tragedy

Seeking favour out of grief
Telling the Indians who is their chief
The pendulum swings from left to right
It matters not who's black or white

Insecure, jealous or just afraid
Neurosis the card that's too often played
Not everyone stakes such an open hand
As clubs are raised and jokers banned

But in this world where all around
Ignorance breeds on fallow ground
This June Sunday morn I'm clear of head
Cos it's Father's Day here which means breakfast in bed.

Enjoying Father's Day breakfast in bed with the Sunday papers and laughing at all the blame-game agendas in current politics. Next up, a family Sunday National Trust stroll as usual. With me carrying the bag, as usual.

July

Stolen moments in the sun
Father and daughter being as one
Into the sea to splash and scream
Sharing a laugh and eating ice cream

Digging holes deep in the sand
Holding a shell in her tiny hand
If only life could stay like this
The wind in her hair and summer's soft kiss

Alas, I know this day must end
Light must fade and clouds descend
So one last time before innocence is lost
To the ways of the world, the count and the cost

One last chance before 'that talk'
For a beachy frolic and a sandy walk
To smile and laugh and to be carefree
Before eyes are opened to what she must see

The tooth fairy and Santa are on shaky ground
As the truth will out to the saddest sound
No longer a child protected from all
That grown-up stuff from beyond the wall

This little princess will open her eyes
To all the half-truths, confusions and lies
So many questions about who, what and how
To dodge and deflect for the here and the now

Bedtime stories will soon disappear
Replaced by teenage angst and fear
No longer her prince's horse will be white
Her happy-ever-afters will come with a fight

The big, bad world will bare its sharp teeth
Biting through shadows from the beach to the heath
All her fairy wishes will be far, far away
When the sun has set on this warm July day.

*Written on the beach at West Wittering, West Sussex.
Feeling melancholic as my daughter played in the sea and
the sun on her last day of innocence before learning about
the birds and the bees.*

August

Life is short but love is sweet
So we try to share with all we meet
To make our mark, to take our stand
To offer our help with outstretched hand

We think we know what makes them tick
We don't pre-judge or shout names that stick
Instead we all try to just get along
Pretending that there is nothing wrong

For we cannot feel the pain inside
That makes their heart cower and hide
We pray and hope that maybe some day
The sun will chase their clouds away
Sadly for some this struggle's too much

Way too deep for a mere mortal's touch
Their spirit is trapped, it cannot break free
From all of the demons we're unable to see

Time, the great healer that softens most blows
Has washed its hands from the face of these woes
And now that they're gone, the clocks will unwind
No memories will fill the void left behind

As branches sway gently in a soft August breeze
There's a chorus of contentment from birds in the trees
And from the chains that have bound, there's a final release
And maybe at last their soul has found peace.

August found me coping with bereavement following a loss on my wife's side of the family and contemplating coming back as a tree when I go.

September

Living in a village can often be quite hard
When folk who know your business play the judge-and-jury
card

You'll see them in the morning when you're running late for work
With tired eyes, still yawning, you beep them from your Merc

They've got no time for small talk, they *must* be on their way
There's a mutual understanding as you start a brand-new day
We've all got stuff that's going on, things that take their toll
Money, schools and health issues, at work or on the dole

We have so many things in common that tie us into one
With children at the forefront of most things that are done
But sadly there are break-ups, where opinions have been split
When foolish pride takes over once the torches have been lit

So is it really that important to fight until you fall?
As time will move you further from whatever started it all
I'm often told to pick a side, to get down from the fence
But if you breathe a little deeper, you'll see it's just common sense

Cos I'll always be consistent, try and see it from both sides
And keep the strictest confidence of anyone who confides
For now it is September and before autumn arrives
Why say something you regret for the rest of your lives?

So hold out far your olive branch, forget what's gone before
Offer the hand of friendship and end your silly war.

September sees us back at the school gates where we learn who has fallen out with who during the summer. But so long as our two are still getting on, there's hope for the world at large!

October

Mother and daughter walking tall
As summer stands aside for fall
For Hallowe'en is now here
Trick or treat but have no fear

Around the corner winter waits
Tinsel glitters on garden gates
As festive cheer spreads all around
Snow will settle on higher ground

But let's not waste our time away
Let's just enjoy every single day
Moments treasured as if the last
Rejoicing memories from the past

Live for now and all you see
Spread your love and empathy
Know what counts in your own life
For father, daughter, son or wife

We all have dreams to live and share
But it's only families who truly care
So tell 'em you love 'em every night
And through their darkness, Always be their light.

Written as my wife and daughter walked the Halloween Trail at Polesden Lacey, Great Bookham, Surrey. Still dealing with bereavement, my daughter is now more aware of her surroundings and the ways of the world. With Christmas coming, this walk highlighted the importance of family union in times of both happiness and heartbreak.

November

Sounds of laughter, and children's cries
As fires light up November's skies
A village unites to be as one
To eat and drink and have some fun

Volunteers rising to the call
For this is the greatest show of all
Extolling virtues and all that's good
Community spirit in this neighbourhood

Health and safety all in hand
Every detail finely planned
And what a night that we all had
Every mother, daughter, son and dad

May the Fawkes be with you and to all good men
As the bonfire rages once again
The conspirators and their effigies
Are set alight to joyful glees

Flashing horns and coloured lights
Chocolate drinks and burger bites
Three cheers for all – you've done so well
As a happy crowd heads to The Bell.

Fireworks night in the village of Fetcham. A great community event with many an ooooh! and many an aaaah! before we, naturally, all disappeared to our local pub, The Bell.

December

For every band that ever was
Or every dream that lives because
Their will to win has never died
No matter however hard they tried

To put you down or kill your soul
Destroy the heart of rock 'n' roll
For every pub that ripped you off
Sneering laugh or sarcastic cough

Ambivalence or attitude
Objects thrown or crowds that booed
Promotors who just won't call back
The 'pay to play' or the media flack

Being judged by the blind insane
When you just play to entertain
Spit and sawdust with no stage
Young or old, it ain't about your age

Punters walk in off the street
Think they own each chord or beat
They ain't paid, so they don't care
You're cannon fodder for their drunken fayre

Reality shows have set the scene
For the karaoke king and queen
With Jäger Bombs held in each hand
No longer do they respect the band

But this December, You'll know who we are
As we unleash hell in every bar
So think before you dare to mock
Cos we are *Ransom* and we know how to Rock!!!

A rallying call to the hardworking bands gigging week in, week out on the pub circuit. At Christmas time, the wannabees, apathists and anarchists take their act up a notch or two. So we crank ours up to... number 11, as I believe they say in Spinal Tap.